Quick & Easy
CROSS STITCH GIFTS

Dorothea Hall

MARK
PUBLISHING

5400 SCOTTS VALLEY DR.
SCOTTS VALLEY, CA 95066

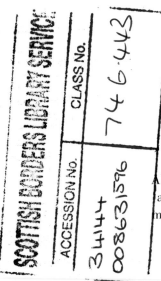
Published 1992 by Merehurst Limited
Ferry House, 51-57 Lacy Road, Putney, London SW15 1PR
© Copyright 1992 Merehurst Limited

ISBN 0-937769-28-2

Distributed in the United States by
Mark Publishing, Inc.
5400 Scotts Valley Drive, Scotts Valley, CA 95066

Edited by Diana Brinton
Designed by Maggie Aldred
Photography by Di Lewis
Illustrations by John Hutchinson
Typesetting by BMD Graphics, Hemel Hempstead
Colour separation by Fotographics Limited, UK – Hong Kong
Printed in Hong Kong by Wing King Tong

*Merehurst is the leading publisher of craft books and has an excellent range
of titles to suit all levels. Please send to the address above for our
free catalogue, stating the title of this book.*

SUPPLIERS

The following mail order
company has supplied
some of the basic items
needed for making up the
projects in this book:

Framecraft Miniatures Limited
148-150 High Street
Aston
Birmingham, B6 4US
England
Telephone (021) 359 4442

*Addresses for Framecraft
worldwide*
Ireland Needlecraft Pty. Ltd.
2-4 Keppel Drive
Hallam, Victoria 3803
Australia

Danish Art Needlework
PO Box 442, Lethbridge
Alberta T1J 3Z1
Canada

Sanyei Imports
PO Box 5, Hashima Shi
Gifu 501-62
Japan

The Embroidery Shop
286 Queen Street
Masterton
New Zealand

Anne Brinkley Designs Inc.
246 Walnut Street
Newton
Mass. 02160
USA

S A Threads and Cottons Ltd.
43 Somerset Road
Cape Town
South Africa

For information on your
nearest stockist of
embroidery cotton,
contact the following:

DMC

USA
The DMC Corporation
Port Kearney Bld.
10 South Kearney
N.J. 07032-0650
Telephone: 201 589 0606

COATS AND ANCHOR

USA
Coats & Clark
P.O. Box 27067
Dept CO1
Greenville
SC 29616
Telephone: 803 234 0103

MADEIRA

U.S.A.
Madeira Marketing Limited
600 East 9th Street
Michigan City
IN 46360
Telephone: 219 873 1000

CONTENTS

INTRODUCTION

One of the delights of cross stitch embroidery is its tremendous versatility – exploited to the full in this range of small gifts, which will hopefully be as pleasurable to make as to receive. Even the smallest designs, such as the Town and Country Mouse paperweights, the simple flower sprig repeated around the Floral Basket Liner and the Magpie, Magpie bookmark demonstrate that small can be both beautiful and quick to produce.

Cross stitch is an extremely easy stitch, and since it is worked over a set number of threads, its appearance is neat and regular, so that with very little practice a beginner can soon embroider quickly and confidently.

Each of these 'quick and easy' designs is carefully charted and colour coded, and is accompanied with full, easy-to-follow instructions for making up the item.

All the designs are easy to cross stitch but some, such as the prepared bookmarks and guest towels, for example, will obviously be quicker to finish, since these items have been specially prepared for embroidery.

Essential finishing techniques, such as binding the scalloped edge of the floral basket liner, are included in the Basic Skills section. This covers everything from preparing and stretching your fabric in either a ring or a frame to mounting your embroidery ready to be displayed.

Every aspect has been covered, thus ensuring that everyone setting out to make these projects will enjoy creating gifts they will be proud to give.

BASIC SKILLS

■

BEFORE YOU BEGIN

PREPARING THE FABRIC
Even with an average amount of handling, many evenweave fabrics tend to fray at the edges, so it is a good idea to overcast the raw edges, using ordinary sewing thread, before you begin.

THE INSTRUCTIONS
Each project begins with a full list of the materials that you will require; Aida, Tula, Lugana and Linda are all fabrics produced by Zweigart. Note that the measurements given for the embroidery fabric include a minimum of 3cm (1¼in) all around to allow for stretching it in a frame and preparing the edges to prevent them from fraying.

A colour key for DMC stranded embroidery cotton is given with each chart. It is assumed that you will need to buy one skein of each colour mentioned, even though you may use less, but where two or more skeins are needed, this information is included in the main list of requirements.

Should you wish to use Coats/Anchor, or Madeira, stranded embroidery cottons, refer to the conversion chart given at the back of the book (page 48).

To work from the charts, particularly those where several symbols are used in close proximity, some readers may find it helpful to have the chart enlarged so that the squares and symbols can be seen more easily. Many photocopying services will do this for a minimum charge.

Before you begin to embroider, always mark the centre of the design with two lines of basting stitches, one vertical and one horizontal, running from edge to edge of the fabric, as indicated by the arrows on the charts.

As you stitch, use the centre lines given on the chart and the basting threads on your fabric as reference points for counting the squares and threads to position your design accurately.

WORKING IN A HOOP
A hoop is the most popular frame for use with small areas of embroidery. It consists of two rings, one fitted inside the other; the outer ring usually has an

adjustable screw attachment so that it can be tightened to hold the stretched fabric in place. Hoops are available in several sizes, ranging from 10cm (4in) in diameter to quilting hoops with a diameter of 38cm (15in). Hoops with table stands or floor stands attached are also available.

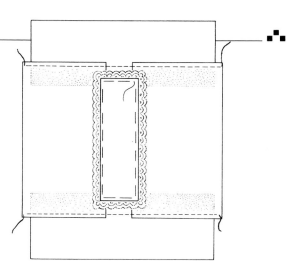

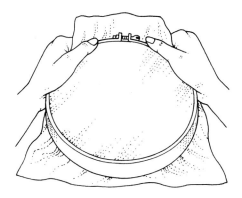

1 To stretch your fabric in a hoop, place the area to be embroidered over the inner ring and press the outer ring over it with the tension screw released. Tissue paper can be placed between the outer ring and the embroidery, so that the hoop does not mark the fabric. Lay the tissue paper over the fabric when you set it in the hoop, then tear away the central, embroidery area.

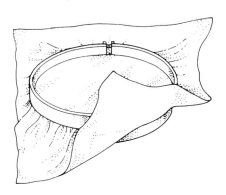

2 Smooth the fabric and, if needed, straighten the grain before tightening the screw. The fabric should be evenly stretched.

EXTENDING EMBROIDERY FABRIC
It is easy to extend a piece of embroidery fabric, such as a bookmark, to stretch it in a hoop.

● Fabric oddments of a similar weight can be used. Simply cut four pieces to size (in other words, to the measurement that will fit both the embroidery fabric and your hoop) and baste them to each side

of the embroidery fabric before stretching it in the hoop in the usual way.

WORKING IN A RECTANGULAR FRAME
Rectangular frames are more suitable for larger pieces of embroidery. They consist of two rollers, with tapes attached, and two flat side pieces, which slot into the rollers and are held in place by pegs or screw attachments. Available in different sizes, either alone or with adjustable table or floor stands, frames are measured by the length of the roller tape, and range in size from 30cm (12in) to 68cm (27in).

As alternatives to a slate frame, canvas stretchers and the backs of old picture frames can be used. Provided there is sufficient extra fabric around the finished size of the embroidery, the edges can be turned under and simply attached with drawing pins (thumb tacks) or staples.

1 To stretch your fabric in a rectangular frame, cut out the fabric, allowing at least an extra 5cm (2in) all around the finished size of the embroidery. Baste a single 12mm (½in) turning on the top and bottom edges and oversew strong tape, 2.5cm (1in) wide, to the other two sides. Mark the centre line both ways with basting stitches. Working from the centre outwards and using strong thread, oversew the top and bottom edges to the roller tapes. Fit the side pieces into the slots, and roll any extra fabric on one roller until the fabric is taut.

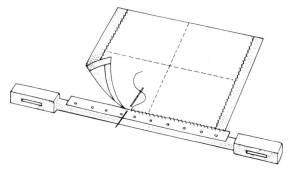

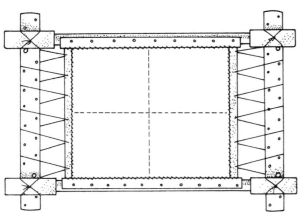

2 Insert the pegs or adjust the screw attachments to secure the frame. Thread a large-eyed needle (chenille needle) with strong thread or fine string and lace both edges, securing the ends around the intersections of the frame. Lace the webbing at 2.5cm (1in) intervals, stretching the fabric evenly.

ENLARGING A GRAPH PATTERN

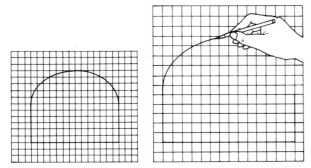

● To enlarge a graph pattern, you will need a sheet of graph paper ruled in 1cm (⅜in) squares, a ruler and pencil. If, for example, the scale is one square to 5cm (2in) you should first mark the appropriate lines to give a grid of the correct size. Copy the graph freehand from the small grid to the larger one, completing one square at a time. Use a ruler to draw the straight lines first, and then copy the freehand curves.

TO BIND AN EDGE

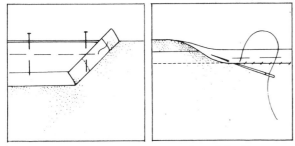

1 Open out the turning on one edge of the bias binding and pin in position on the right side of the fabric, matching the fold to the seamline. Fold over the cut end of the binding. Finish by overlapping the starting point by about 12mm (½in). Baste and machine stitch along the seamline.

2 Fold the binding over the raw edge to the wrong side, baste and, using matching sewing thread, neatly hem to finish.

PIPED SEAMS

Contrasting piping adds a special decorative finish to a seam and looks particularly attractive on items such as cushions and cosies.

You can cover piping cord with either bias-cut fabric of your choice or a bias binding; alternatively, ready-covered piping cord is available in several widths and many colours.

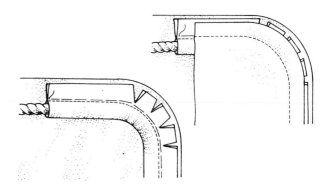

1 To apply piping, pin and baste it to the right side of the fabric, with seam lines matching. Clip into the seam allowance where necessary.

2 With right sides together, place the second piece of fabric on top, enclosing the piping. Baste and then either hand stitch in place or machine stitch, using a zipper foot. Stitch as close to the piping as possible, covering the first line of stitching.

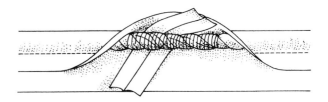

3 To join ends of piping cord together, first overlap the two ends by about 2.5cm (1in). Unpick the two cut ends of bias to reveal the cord. Join the bias strip as shown. Trim and press the seam open. Unravel and splice the two ends of the cord. Fold the bias strip over it, and finish basting around the edge.

MOUNTING EMBROIDERY

The cardboard should be cut to the size of the finished embroidery, with an extra 6mm (¼in) added all around to allow for the recess in the frame.

LIGHTWEIGHT FABRICS

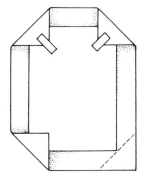 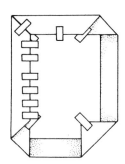

1 Place the emboidery face down, with the cardboard centred on top, and basting and pencil lines matching. Begin by folding over the fabric at each corner and securing it with masking tape.
2 Working first on one side and then the other, fold over the fabric on all sides and secure it firmly with pieces of masking tape, placed about 2.5cm (1in) apart. Also neaten the mitred corners with masking tape, pulling the fabric tightly to give a firm, smooth finish.

HEAVIER FABRICS

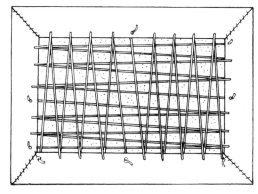

● Lay the embroidery face down, with the cardboard centred on top; fold over the edges of the fabric on opposite sides, making mitred folds at the corners, and lace across, using strong thread. Repeat on the other two sides. Finally, pull up the stitches fairly tightly to stretch the fabric firmly over the cardboard. Overstitch the mitred corners.

CROSS STITCH

For all cross stitch embroidery, the following two methods of working are used. In each case, neat rows of vertical stitches are produced on the back of the fabric.

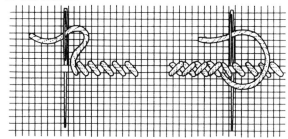

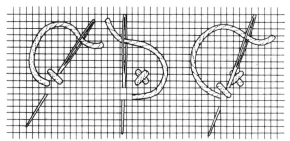

● When stitching large areas, work in horizontal rows. Working from right to left, complete the first row of evenly spaced diagonal stitches over the number of threads specified in the project instructions. Then, working from left to right, repeat the process. Continue in this way, making sure each stitch crosses in the same direction.
● When stitching diagonal lines, work downwards, completing each stitch before moving to the next.

BACKSTITCH

Backstitch is used in the projects to give emphasis to a particular foldline, an outline or a shadow. The stitches are worked over the same number of threads as the cross stitch, forming continuous straight or diagonal lines.

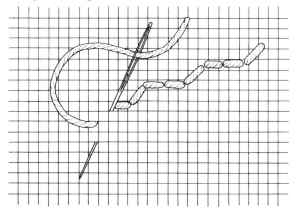

● Make the first stitch from left to right; pass the needle behind the fabric, and bring it out one stitch length ahead to the left. Repeat and continue in this way along the line.

Floral Basket Liner

Embroidered with a simple border of pastel-coloured flowers, this liner, with its pretty scalloped edge, is the perfect accessory for a basket of beautifully-wrapped sweets or petit fours. The edge is bound with a contrasting binding, but you could buttonhole stitch around the edge as an alternative. Embroider the cross stitching first, then the buttonholing; finally, trim the fabric up to the outer twisted edge of the stitching.

FLORAL BASKET LINER

YOU WILL NEED

For a Basket liner, measuring 30cm × 25cm
(12in × 10in):

*34cm × 29cm (13½in × 11½in) of white linen,
28 threads to 2.5cm (1in)
DMC stranded embroidery cotton in the colours
given in the panel
No26 tapestry needle
115cm (1¼yd) of contrast cotton bias binding,
12mm (½in) wide
Sewing thread to match the contrast binding
15cm (6in) square of cardboard for a template
(use a breakfast cereal box, or similar packaging)
Tracing paper*

●

THE EMBROIDERY

Stretch the prepared fabric in a frame and, following the chart, cross stitch the motifs given in one quarter section, as marked by the basting stitches. Use two strands of thread in the needle and work one cross stitch over two threads of fabric throughout. For the remaining three sections, turn the frame through 90 degrees and repeat the cross stitching.

Remember not to strand the thread across the back of the fabric, or it will show through on the right side. Remove the finished embroidery from the frame, retaining the basting stitches, and steam press on the wrong side.

DRAWING THE SCALLOPED EDGE

Using a soft pencil, trace the outline of the quarter section, as shown, and transfer it to the cardboard (to do this, simply turn the tracing over and, placing it on the cardboard, pencil over the back of the outline). Cut out the template.

Lay the embroidery face down and position the template over one quarter section, matching the straight lines to the basted lines. Lightly draw

around the scalloped edge with a pencil. Repeat for the other three quarter sections, cut around the scalloped edge, and remove the basting stitches.

BINDING THE EDGE

With right sides and raw edges together, pin and baste the binding around the edge (see page 6),

To complete the embroidery, turn the fabric through 90 degrees and repeat the design three times.

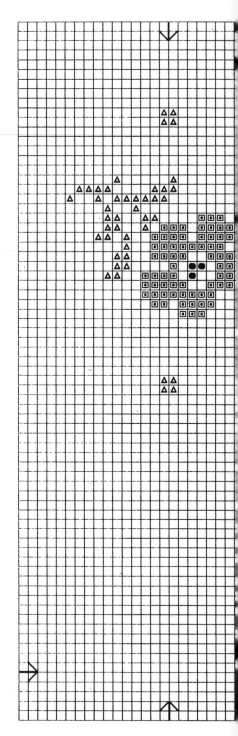

beginning in the corner of one scallop. Where the two ends of the binding meet, overlap by 2cm (¾in), turning the raw, overlapped end under by 6mm (¼in) to neaten it. Using matching sewing thread, machine stitch or backstitch in place.

Turn the binding over the edge of the fabric, and hem, sewing into the back of the first stitching to prevent the thread from showing through.

FLORAL BASKET LINER ▼

↓	725	yellow
✲	961	pink
●	326	dark red
⊡	341	blue
△	733	olive green

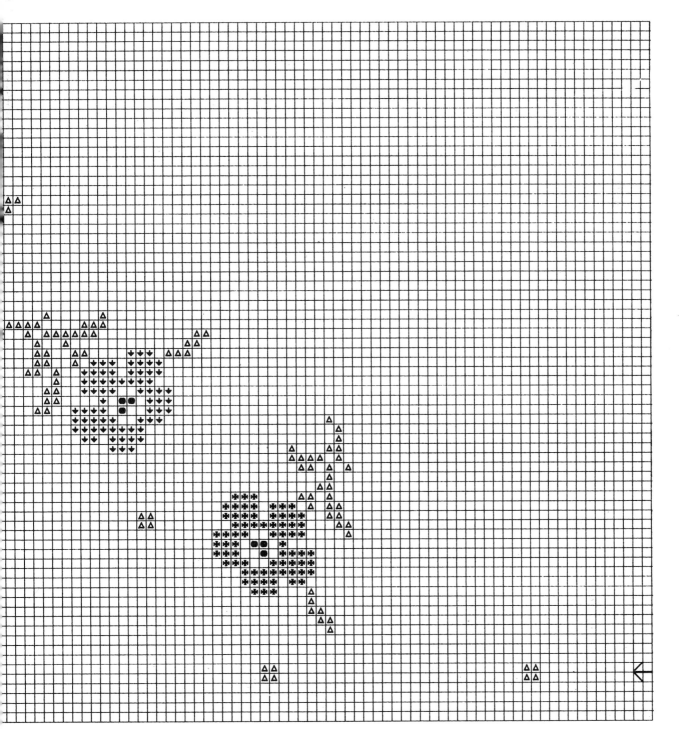

Candle Screen and Bookmark

Embroider this delicate little candle screen, with its eastern imagery, and the accompanying bookmark to evoke days gone by – a timely reminder of the many leisurely hours that people used to spend reading by candlelight. The bookmark, like the candlescreen, is purchased, but you could easily make your own, finishing it with a lacy trim like the one shown in the picture. With its image of a little mermaid, skimming through the water on the back of a dolphin, it would make a delightful complement to an encyclopedia of fairy tales. Alternatively, the streamlined image of the dolphin could perhaps be set into a child's hairband for party occasions.

CANDLE SCREEN

YOU WILL NEED

For a candle screen approximately 46cm (18in)
high with an adjustable screen and design area
12.5 cm × 9cm (4¾ × 3½in):

*20cm × 15cm (8in × 6in) of blue evenweave Aida
fabric, 14 threads to 2.5cm (1in)
DMC stranded embroidery cotton in the colours
given in the appropriate panel
No24 tapestry needle
Wooden candle screen
(for suppliers, see page 2)*

•

THE EMBROIDERY

Mark the centre of the fabric both ways with basting
stitches, and prepare the edges, then stretch it in
a frame (see page 5).

Following the chart, and using two strands of
thread in the needle throughout, complete the cross
stitching, then work the backstitch details on top.

When embroidering this type of scenic design, it
is always a good idea to stitch the foreground, such
as the tree on the left, before the background. And
also, where very light and dark colours are involved
in a design, it is always better to embroider the
lighter colours last of all, to minimize handling, and
the risk of dirtying the thread. Obviously, while
your embroidery is not being worked, it is advisable
to keep it covered up.

Remove the finished embroidery from the frame
and press it on the wrong side.

ASSEMBLING THE CANDLE SCREEN

Mount the embroidery on the supplied card, following the instructions given for lightweight fabrics on
page 7. Follow the manufacturer's instructions to
finish the assembly.

BOOKMARK

YOU WILL NEED

For a bookmark measuring about 25cm × 9cm
(10in × 3½in):

*One ready-made lace-edged cream bookmark with
a Hardanger centre, 16 threads to 2.5cm (1in)
(for suppliers, see page 2)
DMC stranded embroidery cotton in the colours
given in the appropriate panel
No26 tapestry needle*

•

THE EMBROIDERY

Using oddments from your scrap bag, baste small
pieces of fabric to the long edges of the bookmark.
Either stretch it in a hoop, see page 4, or simply
push drawing-pins through the fabric pieces to
attach the work to a canvas stretcher.

There are some professional embroiderers who
prefer to work cross stitch in the hand, and provided you keep an eye on your stitching tension,
this small bookmark may be the exception to the
general rule that it is advisable to hold the work in
a frame of some kind.

With centre lines basted, and following the chart
given opposite, complete the embroidery, using two
strands of thread in the needle throughout.

Remove the basting threads and steam press on
the wrong side.

It would be quite easy to make your own bookmarks for cross stitching, from oddments of evenweave left over from other projects.

You could machine zigzag stitch broderie
anglaise or lace trim around the edges, and on the
lower edge, add a similar ribbon marker in colours
of your choice. These would not only be your own
creation, but would be an inexpensive and econo-
mical way of using up leftovers – and perhaps, a
quick and easy project to make for the next bazaar
you are asked to support!

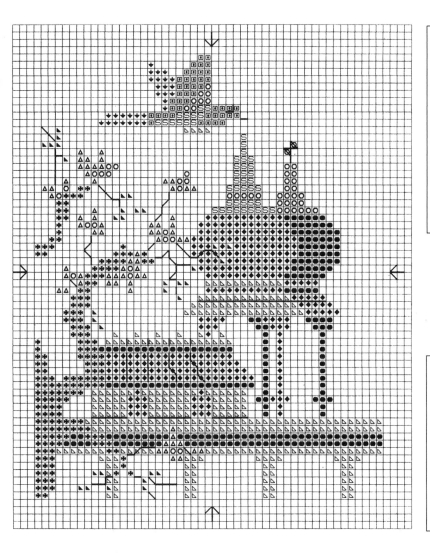

◄ THE NIGHTINGALE

◣ white
S 743 yellow
○ 783 gold
◆ 3713 pink
● 3733 deep pink (bks buildings)
△ 350 red
◣ 563 green
✳ 3768 dark green (bks branches)
⊡ 928 pale grey
↓ 647 grey (bird's eye and beak)

THE MERMAID ▼

❘ 834 yellow
○ 3779 flesh (bks 3354; eye 598)
△ 3354 pink
● 3042 mauve
✳ 452 drab mauve (bks 3042)
◆ 828 pale blue
⊡ 598 turquoise (bks on water)
↓ 928 grey

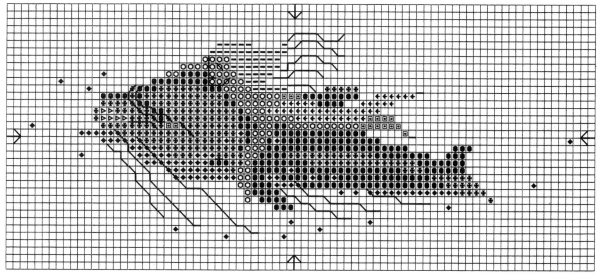

Happy Birthday

Naturalistic flowers and fruits, embroidered on backgrounds of a contrast colour, are featured on this charming trio of birthday greetings cards. Friends and relatives will be delighted to receive them, and cards as pretty as this should be framed after the day and hung as miniature pictures.

HAPPY BIRTHDAY

YOU WILL NEED

For the three Birthday greetings cards, each measuring overall 20cm × 14cm (8in × 5½in), with oval portrait cut outs, 14cm × 9.5cm (5½in × 3¾in):

For the *Rose* card:

23cm × 18cm (9in × 7¼in) of evenweave Linda fabric, 26 threads to 2.5cm (1in), in pale blue No26 tapestry needle

For the *Flower Basket* card:

23cm × 18cm (9in × 7¼in) of evenweave Linda fabric, 26 threads to 2.5cm (1in), in yellow No26 tapestry needle

For the *Strawberries* card:

23cm × 18cm (9in × 7¼in) of offwhite linen, 20 threads to 2.5cm (1in) No18 tapestry needle

For each card:

DMC stranded embroidery cotton in the colours given in the appropriate panel Card mount (for suppliers, see page 2)

•

THE EMBROIDERY

Prepare the fabric (overcasting the edges and basting the centre both ways) and then stretch it in a hoop, see page 4. For all three designs, work one cross stitch over two threads of fabric. For the Flower Basket and Rose designs, embroider with two strands of thread in the No26 needle throughout. For the Strawberries design, use the No18 needle and three strands of thread throughout. Embroider the stems first, and then the strawberries and leaves.

Steam press the finished embroideries on the wrong side. Leave the basting stitches in place at this stage; they will be used later for centring the design in the card.

ASSEMBLING THE CARDS

Open out the self-adhesive card mount; centre your embroidery over the cut-out window (using the basting threads as accurate guide lines), and trim the fabric until it is some 12mm (½in) larger all around than the marked area on the card. Remove the basting stitches. Reposition your embroidery; fold over the left-hand section of the card, and press to secure.

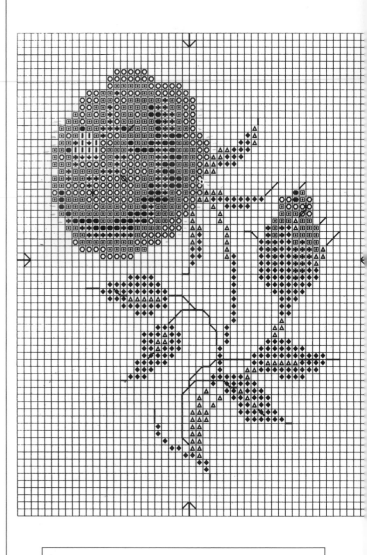

ROSE ▲		
I 734 pale yellow	✚	602 magenta
↓ 972 yellow	◆	966 green
○ 605 pale pink		(bks 959)
⊡ 962 pink	△	959 veridian
● 335 warm pink		green (and bks stems)

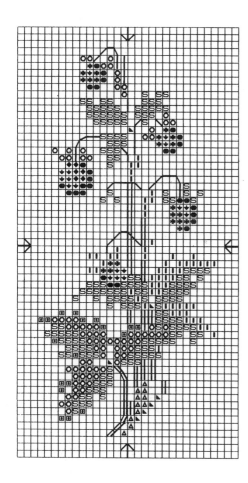

FLOWER BASKET ▼

Symbol	Code	Color
◺	741	yellow
◆	721	orange
⊡	781	ginger (and bks on right side of basket base)
I	761	(bks 3733) pale pink
✺	3733	pink
●	603	pale magenta
△	351	warm pink
↓	341	blue
S	3348	pale green
○	3364	green (and bks stems)
↑	3047	light stone (bks 781)
◣	372	stone (and bks around basket base, left side and top edge)

STRAWBERRIES ▲

Symbol	Code	Color
◆	776	pale pink
↓	891	pink
✺	350	red
●	817	dark red
S	3348	green
I	3347	sap green
○	937	dark green (and bks curved stems)
⊡	301	ginger
△	975	brown
◣	3045	dark brown (and bks all lower and upright stems – two lines)

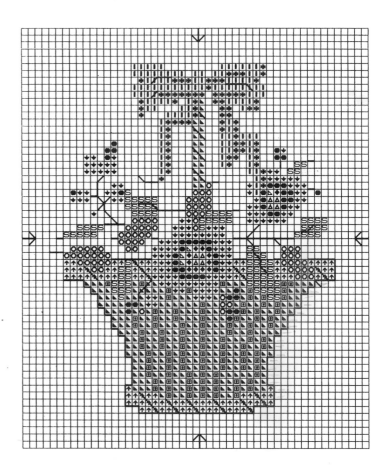

Wall Mirror and Miniature Pictures

'Mirror, mirror on the wall!' – this
delightful wall mirror could be the
starting point for a collection
of silhouettes.
All three items are simple to stitch,
using only one colour, and would
make a lovely gift for a young girl.
If you were adding to the collection,
you might consider stitching a
silhouette of the child herself –
perhaps copying from a photograph.

WALL MIRROR AND MINIATURE PICTURES

YOU WILL NEED

For a wooden wall mirror with an overall measurement of 39.5cm × 13cm (15½ × 5in) and a cross stitch area of 13cm × 9cm (5in × 3½in), and two brass-framed miniatures each measuring 10cm (4in) in diameter:

60cm × 20cm (24in × 8in) of pale blue evenweave Aida fabric, 16 threads to 2.5cm (1in)
DMC stranded embroidery cotton: 3 skeins of 3350
No26 tapestry needle
Wall mirror and two miniature picture frames
(for suppliers, see page 2)

•

THE EMBROIDERY

You can either stitch all three designs with the single piece of fabric stretched in a rectangular frame, or use a hoop for the individual designs. Whichever you decide, first divide the fabric into three equal sections, each measuring 20cm (8in) square, either cutting the fabric or marking the divisions with basting stitches. Baste the centre both ways on each section, ready for the embroidery. Referring to the charts and, using two strands of the thread in the needle, complete the cross stitching.

Remove from the frame and, if needed, steam press the finished embroidery on the wrong side. Cut out each section along the dividing lines.

ASSEMBLING THE MIRROR AND PICTURES

For the mirror, mount the embroidery following the instructions given on page 7. Complete the assembly, following the manufacturer's instructions.
For the miniature pictures, first place the circular card template over the chart and mark the centre both ways, using a soft pencil. Lay the embroidery face down with the card on top, matching basting stitches and lines, and draw around the card with

pencil. Working freehand, draw a second line about 4cm (1½in) outside, and cut out along this outer line.

With double sewing thread in the needle, make a line of running stitches about 2cm (¾in) in from the raw edge, close to the marked line. Place the card on the wrong side and pull up the thread, spacing the gathers evenly, and making sure the fabric grain is straight. Secure the thread firmly. Add pieces of masking tape over the edges of the fabric for extra strength.

Finish the assembly, following the manufacturer's instructions.

SNOW WHITE AND THE SEVEN DWARFS ▼ MIRROR

● 3350 (and bks details)

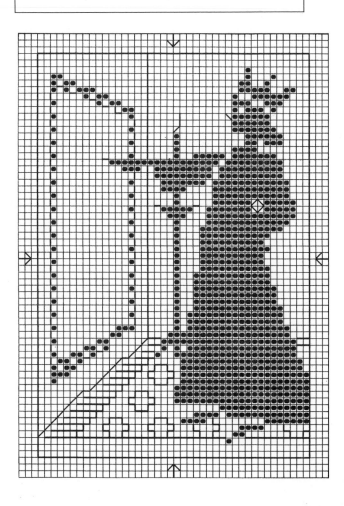

MINIATURE PICTURE ▼

● 3350 (and bks details)

MINIATURE PICTURE ▲

● 3350 (and bks details)

Paper-weights

Made from small remnants of linen, these charming little paperweights are perfect starting points for beginners. Featuring those two well-known opposites, the sophisticated town mouse and the simple country mouse, they would make ideal designs for a child to stitch, perhaps as a gift for a grandmother or a favourite aunt. Alternatively, the two designs, set in either brass or silvered frames, would make a pretty pair of pictures for a small child's room.

PAPERWEIGHTS

YOU WILL NEED

For two paperweights, one an oval measuring
10cm × 8cm (4in × 3in), and the other circular,
measuring 9cm (3½in) in diameter:

25cm × 15cm (10in × 6in) of natural linen,
21 threads to 2.5cm (1in)
DMC stranded embroidery cotton in the colours
given in the appropriate panel
No26 tapestry needle
Glass-topped paperweights
(for suppliers, see page 2)

THE EMBROIDERY

If you are embroidering both designs on one piece
of fabric, begin by preparing the edges and stretching it in a rectangular frame. Otherwise, divide the
fabric in half, overcast the edges, and set each
piece in a hoop.

Baste the centre both ways for each design.
Following the charts and colour keys given opposite, complete the embroidery, using two strands of
thread in the needle throughout. Work the cross
stitching first and then finish with the backstitch
details. Remember when embroidering on very
openweave fabric not to strand across the back,
otherwise the threads will be visible on the right
side. Remove the finished embroidery from the
frame and steam press on the wrong side.

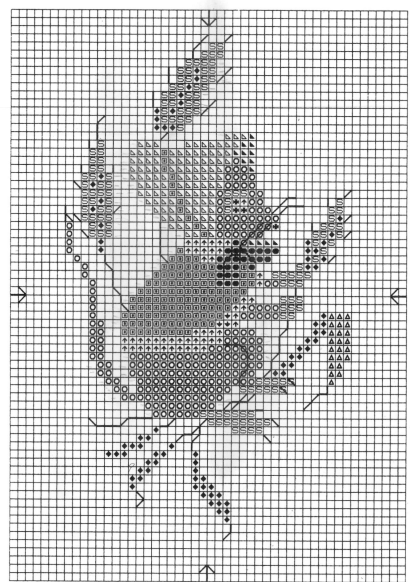

COUNTRY MOUSE ▶

↑ white
S 3046 straw (bks feet)
◣ 224 pink
● 3731 deep pink
◺ 828 pale turquoise
⊡ 518 deep turquoise
△ 3053 sap green (bks leaves)
○ 3045 brown (bks 413)
◆ 772 stone (bks corn stems and
　　whiskers)
↓ 762 grey
✹ 413 dark grey (bks whiskers)

MOUNTING FABRIC OVER A PAPER TEMPLATE

The manufacturer suggests mounting the cut-out embroidery and securing it underneath with the felt backing supplied. This is a suitable method for fine fabrics, but with a medium-weight linen, the raw edges can clearly be seen, giving a slightly frayed look. To overcome this, simply mount the fabric over the paper template supplied.

Place the paper template over the chart and mark the centre both ways, using a soft pencil. Lay the embroidery face down with the template on top, matching basting stitches and centre lines. Draw around the edge with the pencil. Working freehand, draw a second line about 2.5cm (1in) outside, and cut out along this line.

Using sewing thread in the needle, make a line of running stitches about 12mm (½in) in from the raw edge. Place the paper template on the wrong side and pull up the thread, spacing the gathers evenly, and making sure the grain of the fabric is straight and the design is centred.

ASSEMBLING THE PAPERWEIGHTS

Following the instructions given for the Drinks Tray on page 43, mount the embroidery, and then finish the assembly, according to manufacturer's instructions.

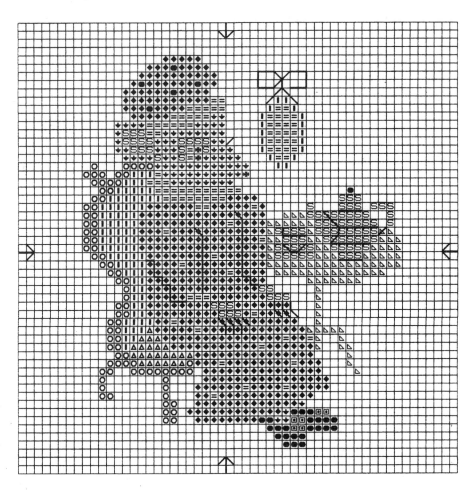

◀ TOWN MOUSE

=	white
◺	3046 straw (bks mirror bow)
⊆	224 pink (bks fingers)
●	3731 deep pink (bks on teaset)
◆	598 turquoise (bks 413)
⊡	518 deep turquoise
△	3053 sap green
○	3045 brown
Ɩ	772 stone
✦	762 grey
✱	413 dark grey (bks eye)

Pretty Pincushions

Pincushions are an essential tool for needleworkers and these three are quick to make and roomy enough to hold a good supply of pins.

One embroidery is set into a purchased cushion on a wooden base, making an attractive gift that might well be left out on display when not in use.

The other two are made like miniature cushions and trimmed, one with simple ribbon bows and the other with fine cord. They would make ideal gifts to bring as a contribution to a fund-raising effort, such as a Christmas crafts fair.

The cord binding was purchased but could have been made from embroidery cotton. To do this, simply cut several long strands; tie them together at one end and secure this to a door handle; twist the other end until the strands are twisted along their entire length, and then hold the centre and bring the two ends together to complete the cord.

PRETTY PINCUSHIONS

YOU WILL NEED

For the *Two Birds* pincushion, measuring
11.5cm (4½in) across:

*18cm (7¼in) square of cream evenweave
Hardanger, 16 threads to 2.5cm (1in)
DMC stranded embroidery cotton in the colours
given in the appropriate panel
No 24 tapestry needle
Pincushion mould with wooden surround
(for suppliers, see page 2)*

For the *Little Maiden* pincushion, measuring
13cm (5in) square:

*Two 15cm (6in) squares of cream evenweave
(Aida) fabric, 14 threads to 2.5cm (1in)
110cm (1⅓yds) of pale pink parcel ribbon
DMC stranded embroidery cotton in the colours
given in the appropriate panel
No 24 tapestry needle
Sufficient kapok or sheep's wool for filling
Matching sewing thread*

For *Wee Willie Winkie* pincushion, measuring
13cm (5in) square:

*Two 15cm (6in) squares of grey evenweave
(Aida 705) fabric, 18 threads to 2.5cm (1in)
60cm (24in) of narrow, deep turquoise cord
DMC stranded embroidery cotton in the colours
given in the appropriate panel
No 26 tapestry needle
Sufficient kapok or sheep's wool for filling
Matching sewing threads*

•

THE EMBROIDERY

Work all three pincushions in the following way.
Prepare the fabric and stretch it in a hoop, see page
4, and taking one of the two squares only for the
Little Maiden and Wee Willie Winkie. Complete
the embroidery, using two strands of thread in the
needle. Remove from the frame and steam press on
the wrong side.

MAKING UP THE PINCUSHIONS

For the *Two Birds* cushion, lay the fabric face down,
with the wooden base centred on top, and draw
around with a soft pencil. Add at least a further
12mm (½in) outside the line and cut out. Run a
gathering thread along the pencil line; centre the
embroidery over the mould, and pin to hold. Pull
up the gathering thread; even out the gathers
around the underside of the mould, and secure the
thread firmly. Attach the mould to the base with the
screw provided.

For the *Little Maiden* and *Wee Willie Winkie*
cushions, in each case place the two sections right
sides together, and then pin and machine stitch
around the edge, taking 12mm (½in) seams and
leaving an 8cm (3in) opening in one side. Turn right
side out and insert the filling. Slipstitch the opening
to close.

For the *Little Maiden*, cut the ribbon into four
equal lengths and tie a bow around each corner,
taking the ribbon twice around before tying. For
Wee Willie Winkie, slipstitch the cord around the
edge, looping the cord into a circle approximately
12mm (½in) in diameter at each corner, as shown
in the photograph.

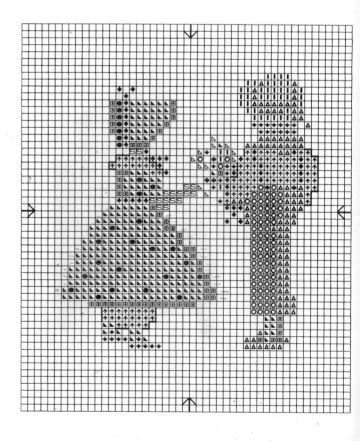

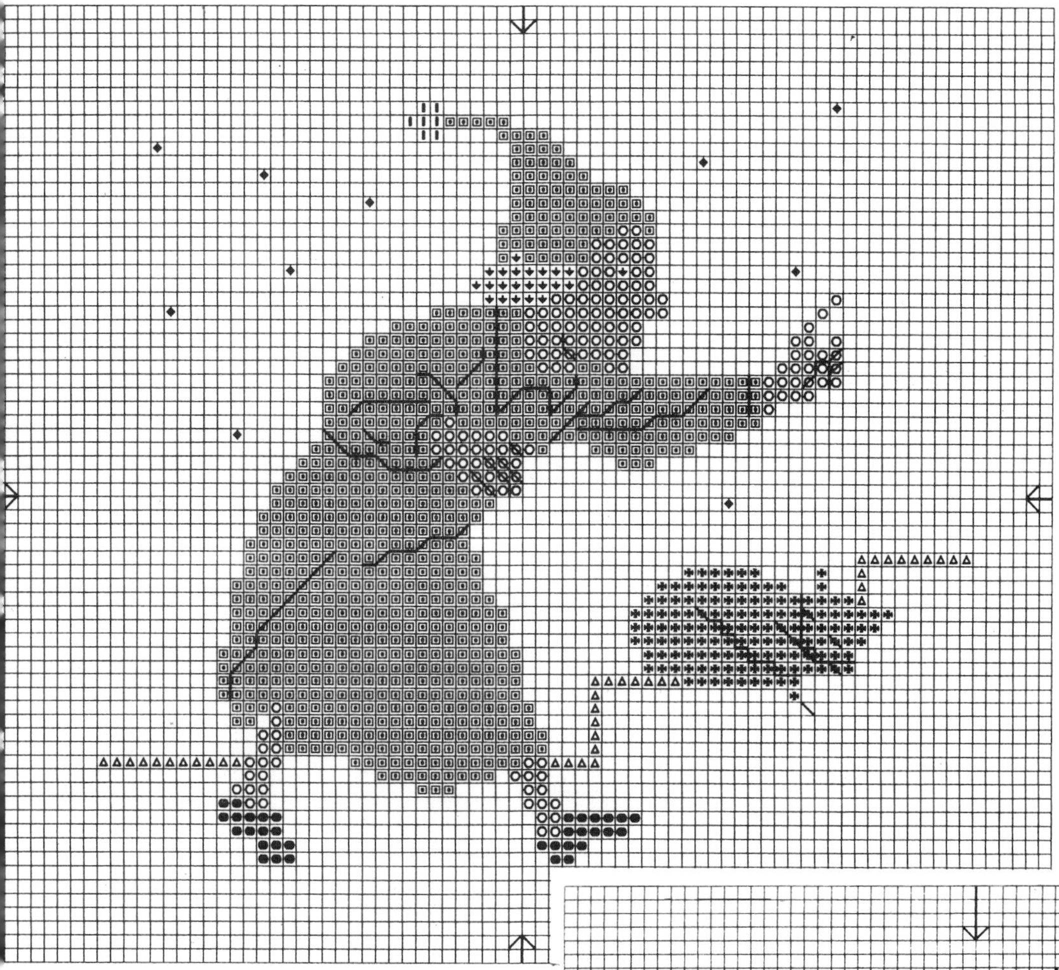

TWO BIRDS ▼

- ◺ white
- ◣ 444 yellow
- △ 3733 pale pink
- ⊡ 893 deep pink
- ○ 3761 pale pink
- ✚ 334 blue (bks bird's feet, small bird's head and body)
- ● 322 dark blue (bks eye, small bird's wings)
- S 471 green (bks tree and ground)
- ↓ 912 veridian green
- I 3756 pale grey

WEE WILLIE WINKIE ▲

- ◆ 444 yellow
- ↓ 680 ochre
- ○ 948 flesh (and bks 224*)
- ● 899 pink
- ⊡ 3761 pale blue (bks 807)
- I 807 blue
- △ 644 stone
- ✚ 413 dark grey (and bks 318*)

*Note: 2 additional backstitch colours**

LITTLE MAIDEN ◀

- ↑ white (bks bloomers and collar 471, bks boy's shirt 799)
- I 834 straw
- S 948 flesh
- ◣ 605 pale pink
- ⊡ 3731 pink
- ● 602 deep pink
- ✚ 892 red
- ○ 3766 light blue
- △ 799 blue
- ◺ 3348 bright green
- ◆ 471 green
- ↓ 3011 brown

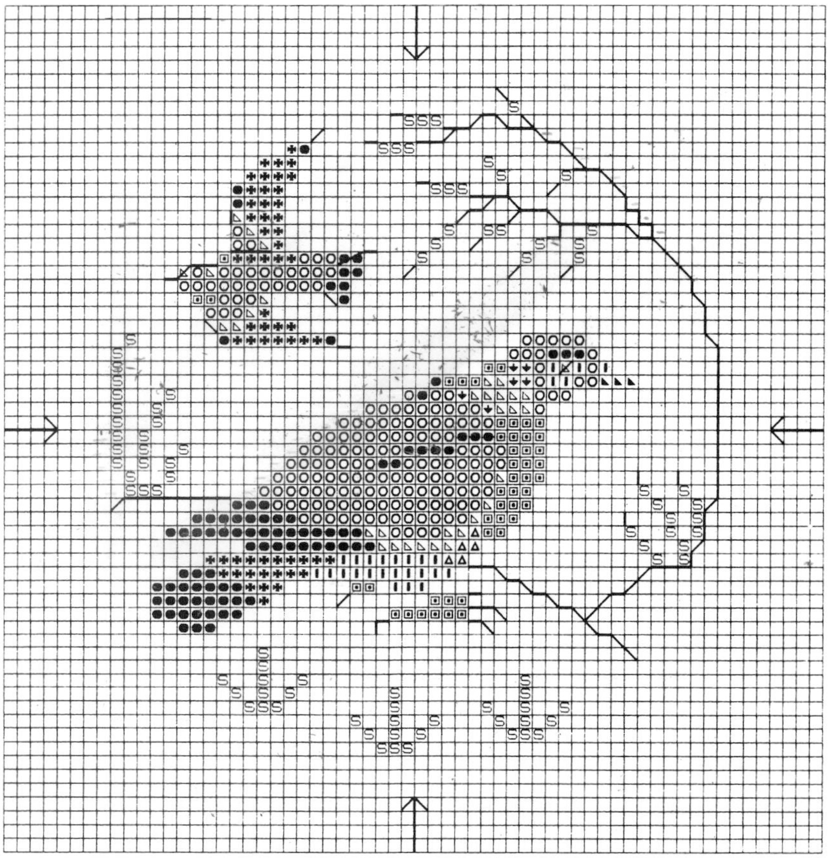

Preserve Pot Covers

Made from washable cotton, these pretty, lace-edged covers are quick and easy to embroider, and will enhance either home-made or store purchased preserves, such as chutneys, mustards, ketchups or pickles.

If you do not have a small embroidery hoop, set a piece of spare fabric in your hoop and secure the pot cover to the centre, stitching around the edge of the inner circle. Taking care not to cut the cover, remove the backing fabric from behind the circle.

PRESERVE-POT COVERS

YOU WILL NEED

For three preserve-pot covers, each measuring 18cm (7¼in) across, with a 6.5cm (2½in) central circle of evenweave Hardanger:

Three lace-edged pot covers with cream evenweave centres, 18 threads to 2.5cm (1in) (for suppliers, see page 2)
210cm (2⅓yd) of bright pink satin ribbon, 6mm (¼in) wide
DMC stranded emboidery cotton in the colours given in the panels
No26 tapestry needle
Ribbon threader

THE EMBROIDERY

These would make lovely beginner's projects for a child wanting to learn cross stitch. So that they are easy to follow, the charts are shown to a large scale.

All three covers are worked in the same way. With the Hardanger placed centrally in a 10cm (4in) diameter hoop (see page 4), and the centre lines based both ways, you can now begin the embroidery. Following the appropriate chart, complete the cross stitching, using two strands of thread in the needle throughout. Use a single strand to work the backstitching on the mouse's body, the twigs carried by the bird and the hair and tail of the sausage.

Remove the basting stitches and steam press the finished covers on the wrong side.

Cut the ribbon into three equal lengths and, using the ribbon threader, thread it through the holes provided in the lace edging.

THE MOUSE ▶

▷ 834 yellow
S 680 ochre
◆ 224 pink
⊡ 3772 brick red
◣ 800 pale blue
I 415 grey (bks 317, including feet)
△ 317 dark grey (bks on bird and water carriers)

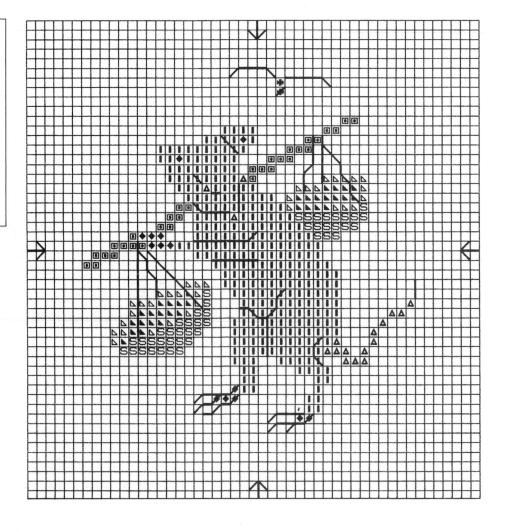

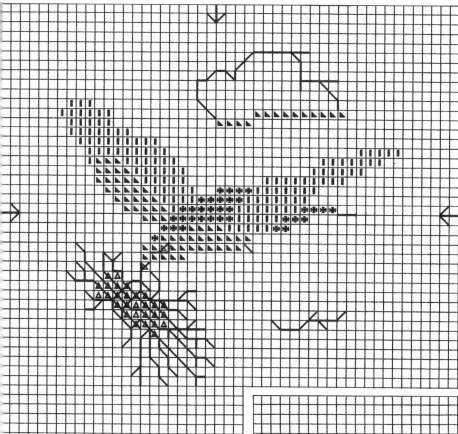

THE BIRD ◀

- △ 834 yellow
- ◣ 800 pale blue (bks on cloud; bks 826)
- ✳ 826 blue
- | 415 grey
- △ 317 dark grey (and bks twigs 3772*)

*Note: one additional backstitch colour**

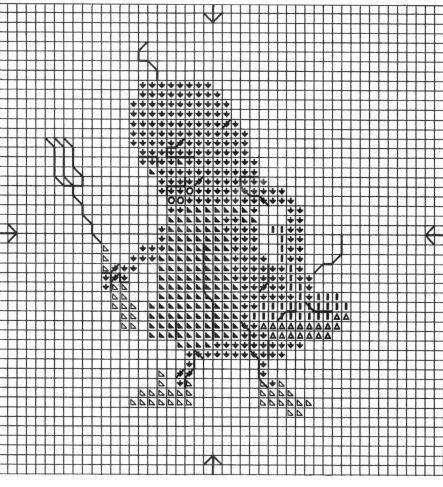

THE SAUSAGE ▶

- △ 834 yellow
- ↓ 224 pink (and bks 3328*)
- ○ 3328 red
- ◣ 800 pale blue (bks 826)
- | 415 pale grey (bks 317)
- △ 317 dark grey (bks fork prongs)

*Note: one additional back stitch colour**, plus 826 also used for The Bird*

Bordered Guest Towels

Plain linen guest towels are decorated with simple floral motifs, repeated in sequence across one short edge only. Instead of embroidering across the full width, you may prefer to stitch a single motif in each corner of the towel.

To embroider other towelling, first cross stitch the design on a band of evenweave fabric and then hem it in place over the towelling pile.

BORDERED
GUEST TOWELS

YOU WILL NEED

For two Guest towels, each measuring
62cm × 37cm (24½in × 14½in):

*Two prepared guest towels, 26 threads to
2.5cm (1in), which can be purchased from
specialist suppliers (see page 2); alternatively, for
applying a band to thick-pile towelling, you will
need evenweave fabric, such as Linda, with
26 threads to 2.5cm (1in), the width of the towel
by 8cm (3in) deep, plus turnings on all sides
DMC stranded embroidery cotton in the colours
given in the panels
No26 tapestry needle
Matching sewing thread for applied band
Narrow lace edging (optional)*

•

THE EMBROIDERY

Embroidering a prepared guest towel is a relatively
easy operation, especially with these repeated
motifs – the most important consideration is to
make sure that you balance the repeats correctly,
starting from the centre.

At the end of the towel to be embroidered, begin
by basting the centre vertically (either count the
threads or measure precisely, and mark with a pin).
The line should ideally be about 15cm (6in) long.
Next, baste the base line across the towel, placing
this line 6cm (2½in) up from the hemstitching of
the fringed edge.

On both designs, work one cross stitch over two
threads of ground fabric. Following the chart and
using two strands of thread in the needle throughout, complete the first half of the border, beginning
in the marked centre. Complete the second half by
repeating the design, again stitching out from the
centre. If you work this way, the finished border
design will be symmetrically balanced out from the
centre, and you will have the same number of
unworked threads at each side.

APPLYING A BAND

Use this technique for decorating purchased towels.
Embroider the design on the evenweave band in
exactly the same way as for a prepared towel. Steam
press the embroidery on the wrong side, and then
make 12mm (½in) turnings all around, and baste.

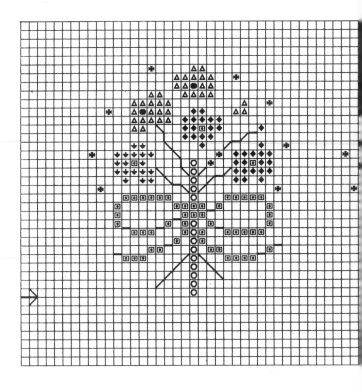

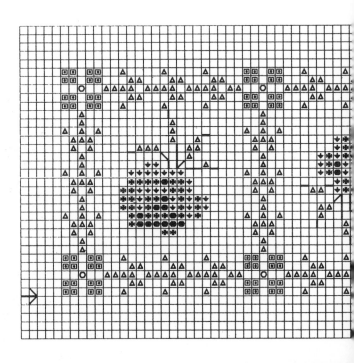

Pin and baste the band to the right side of the towel, 6cm (2½in) up from the lower edge. You may wish to insert a narrow lace edging between the band and the towel, to soften the edge. Machine stitch in place, using matching sewing thread. Remove the basting stitches and steam press to finish.

Centre

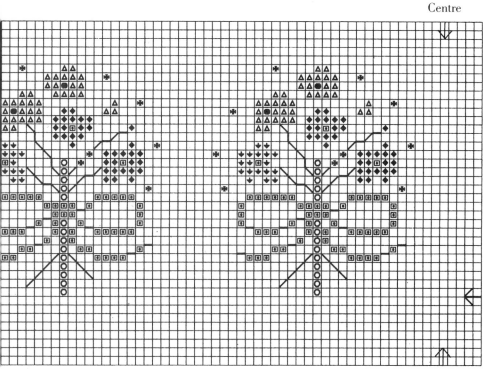

FLORAL BORDER ◄

↓	726	yellow
◆	741	orange
△	721	rust
⊡	3755	blue
●	792	deep blue
✱	959	mint green
○	704	green (and bks stems)

To complete each border, repeat the design working outwards from the centre.

Centre

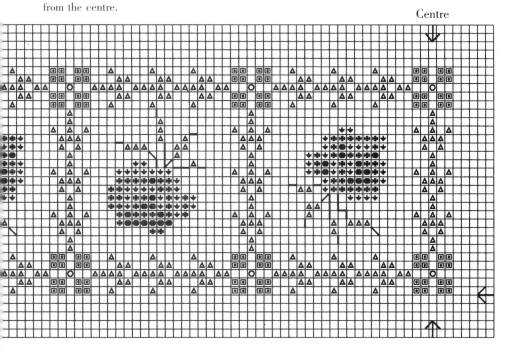

ROSE BORDER ◄

○	726	yellow
↓	818	pale pink
✱	776	pink
●	604	deep pink
⊡	341	blue
△	563	green

39

Drinks Tray

Based on the old rhyme 'Boys and girls come out to play, the moon doth shine as bright as day', this attractive oval drinks tray would make a lovely present for a Christmas or birthday, or perhaps to mark a special occasion, such as retirement.

If this cheerful picture seems wasted when destined to be half hidden under cups or mugs, you might prefer to set it into an oval picture frame, perhaps opting for a coloured background fabric.

COME OUT TO PLAY ▲

- ⊟ white (bks 926)
- ÷ 832 gold
- ↑ 225 flesh (bks 3354)
- ✳ 3354 pink
- ● 3350 deep pink
- = 598 blue (bks 926)
- ◆ 733 olive
- ↓ 731 dark olive
- S 422 buff
- ⊡ 831 brown
- I 926 grey blue
- ◣ 924 dark grey blue
- ○ 3024 light grey (bks 535)
- △ 535 dark grey

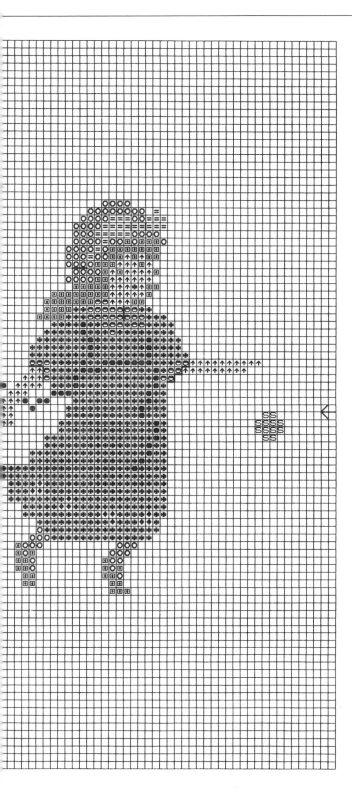

DRINKS TRAY

YOU WILL NEED

For a tray measuring 33cm × 20.5cm
(13in × 8in) with a 28.5cm × 16cm
(11¼in × 6¼in) oval cut out:

*40cm × 30cm (16in × 12in) of cream evenweave
(Aida) fabric, 14 threads to 2.5cm (1in)
DMC stranded embroidery cotton in the colours
given in the panel shown opposite
No24 tapestry needle
33cm × 20.5cm (13in × 8in) of lightweight
iron-on interfacing
Oval wooden tray (for suppliers, see page 2)*

•

THE EMBROIDERY

Begin by stretching the prepared fabric in an embroidery frame (see page 5). Then, following the colour key and chart, complete the cross stitching, using two strands of thread in the needle throughout. Remove the embroidery from the frame and, if necessary, steam press it on the wrong side. Do not remove the basting stitches at this stage.

ASSEMBLING THE TRAY

Using a soft pencil, mark the mounting card (supplied with the tray) both ways along the centre.

Lay the embroidery face down on a clean surface. Centre the card over it, with the pencil lines and basting stitches matching, and lightly draw around the card outline, using the pencil. Remove the basting threads, carefully cut out the embroidery, and back it with the lightweight iron-on interfacing. Alternatively, trim the fabric to leave a 4cm (1½in) allowance, and run a gathering thread around 12mm (½in) away from the pencil line. Position the card and pull up the gathers evenly. Either lace across the back or secure the edges with masking tape.

Follow the manufacturer's instructions to complete the assembly of your tray.

Trim Bookmarks

Here are bookmarks to please any reader. Each has a motif delicately edged with lace and a ribbon rosette or with loop stitch and a fine cotton tassel.

Relatively quick and simple to make, any of these would make a cheering and thoughtful present for a bedridden or chair-bound invalid, and a welcome change from fruit or flowers.

Two of the designs are embroidered on specially purchased bookmarks, while the central marker, featuring the two magpies, is stitched on a handmade example.

Bookmarks inevitably take a considerable amount of wear and handling, and can become rather grubby, so it might be a good idea to protect your finished embroidery by spraying with a proprietory dirt repellant.

TRIM BOOKMARKS

YOU WILL NEED

For the *Mary's Canary* and *The Ten O'clock Scholar* bookmarks, each measuring about 25cm (10in) long:

One cream and one white prepared lace-edged bookmark, 18 threads to 2.5cm (1in), each bookmark 5cm (2in) wide (for suppliers, see page 2)
DMC stranded embroidery cotton in the colours given in the appropriate panel
No26 tapestry needle

For the *Magpie, Magpie* bookmark, also about 25cm (10in) long:

23cm (9in) of white evenweave prepared braid, 5cm (2in) wide, 15 threads to 2.5cm (1in)
DMC stranded embroidery cotton in the colours given in the appropriate panels
No24 tapestry needle
Matching sewing thread

•

THE EMBROIDERY

Working in an embroidery hoop (see page 4 for the instructions on how to stretch small pieces of fabric in a frame) and with basted centre lines, complete the embroidery, using two strands of thread in the needle throughout.

Remove the basting stitches and, if needed, steam press on the wrong side.

FINISHING THE MAGPIE BOOKMARK

Make a small double turning on the top edge and, with matching thread, hem in place.

To make a point on the lower edge, fold the bookmark lengthways in half with the wrong side facing out and backstitch the short edges together. Trim the corner, press the seam open and turn to the right side. Flatten out the bookmark, thus creating a point. Press on the wrong side, and slipstitch to hold.

Make the tassel by winding ordinary white basting thread around a piece of card about 3cm (1¼in) wide. Thread the end into a needle, slip off the tassel threads and bind the loose thread several times around the bunch, close to the top. Pass the needle up through the binding so that it comes out at the top of the tassel – ready to be sewn to the point.

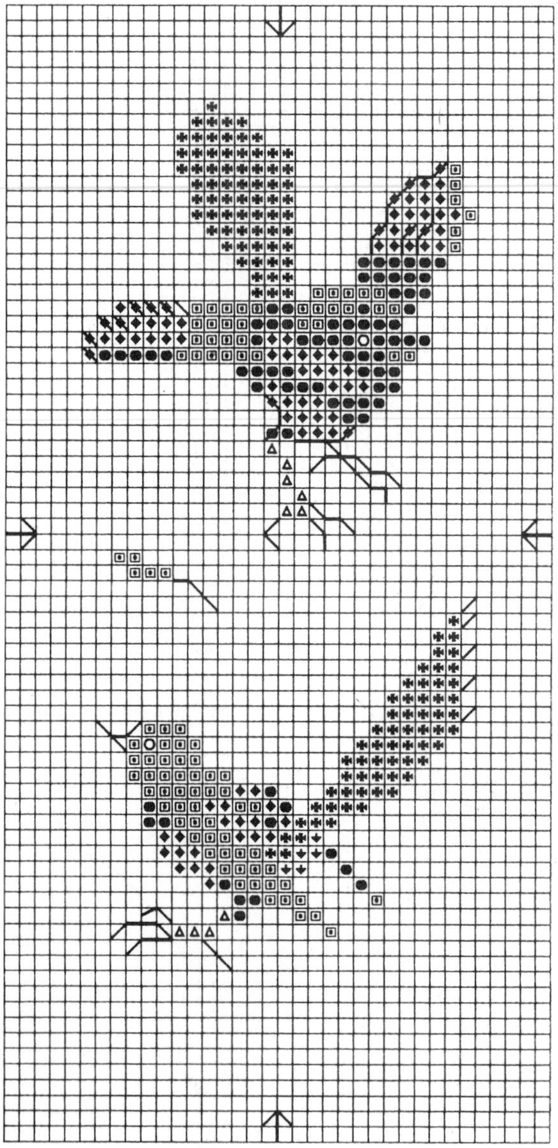

MAGPIE, MAGPIE ▲

◆ white (bks wings 312, body 823)
○ 472 gold
⊡ 312 blue
● 823 dark blue
△ 3052 olive (bks feet)
↓ 937 green
✚ 904 dark green

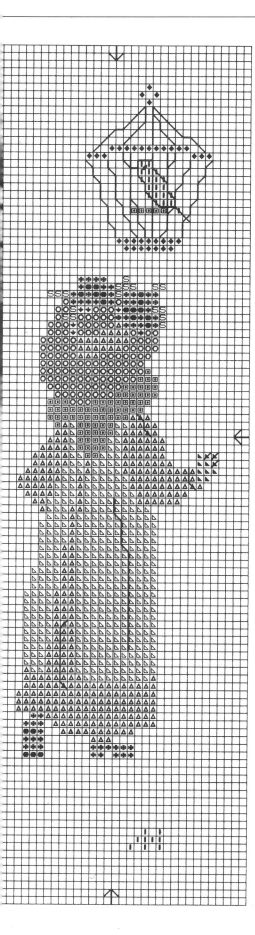

MARY'S CANARY ◀

- ◣ 948 flesh (bks 3326)
- I 445 pale yellow
- ◺ 727 yellow (bks 833)
- ✚ 783 orange
- ○ 833 ochre
- ✳ 3326 pink
- ● 335 deep pink
- △ 794 blue (bks 988)
- S 913 green
- ◆ 988 dark green
- ⊡ 3011 dark brown

TEN O'CLOCK SCHOLAR ▶

- ◣ white (and bks 415*)
- I 948 flesh
- ✳ 968 pink (bks 3766)
- ○ 3766 sea green (bks 931)
- ● 931 deep blue green
- ◆ 738 straw
- ✚ 435 brown
- △ 612 drab brown
- ⊡ 611 dark brown

*Note: one additional backstitch colour**

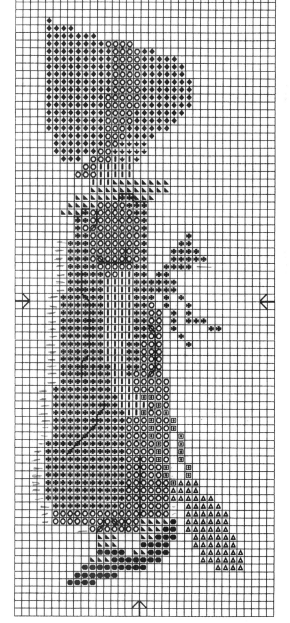

ACKNOWLEDGEMENTS

The author would like to offer her grateful thanks to the following people who helped with the cross stitching of projects in this book with such skill and enthusiasm: Gisela Banbury, Clarice Blakey, Caroline Davies, Christina Eustace, Janet Grey, Anne Whitbourn, and to Julie Hasler for her designs — Wee Willie Winkie page 28 and Ten o'clock Scholar page 44.
Thanks are also due to DMC Creative World Ltd for providing the black and white charts.

CONVERSION CHART

Not all of these colour conversions are exact matches, and bracketed numbers are given as close substitutes.

DMC	ANCHOR	COATS	MADEIRA	DMC	ANCHOR	COATS	MADEIRA	DMC	ANCHOR	COATS	MADEIRA
White	2	1001	White	704	(256)	6238	1308	928	(900)	7225	1709
224	893	3241	0813	725	(306)	2298	0108	931	(921)	7051	1711
225	892	3006	0814	726	295	2294	0109	937	268	—	1504
301	(349)	—	2306	727	293	—	0110	948	(778)	2331	0306
312	(147)	7979	1005	731	(281)	—	1613	958	187	6186	1114
317	(400)	8512	1714	733	(280)	—	1611	959	186	6185	1113
318	(399)	8511	1802	734	(279)	—	1610	961	40	—	0610
322	(978)	7978	1004	738	942	5375	2013	962	52	—	0609
326	(59)	3401	0508	741	304	2314	0201	966	206	—	1209
334	161	7977	1003	743	(297)	2302	0113	972	303	—	0107
335	(42)	3283	0506	761	(8)	3068	0404	988	(257)	6258	1402
349	13	2335	0212	762	397	8510	1804	3011	856	—	1607
350	(11)	3011	0213	772	(264)	6250	1604	3024	(391)	8390	1901
351	(10)	3012	0214	776	(24)	3281	0503	3042	869	4221	0807
368	(261)	6016	1310	781	308	—	2213	3045	(888)	—	2103
372	(88)	—	2210	794	120	—	0907	3046	887	2410	2206
413	401	8514	1713	798	(131)	7022	0911	3047	(886)	2300	2205
415	398	8510	1803	799	(130)	7030	0910	3052	(844)	—	1509
422	(373)	5372	2102	800	(128)	—	0908	3053	(859)	6315	1510
435	(365)	5371	2010	807	(168)	—	1109	3326	(26)	3126	0504
452	—	—	1807	818	48	3281	0502	3328	(11)	3071	0408
471	(280)	—	1501	823	150	—	1008	3347	267	6266	1408
472	253	—	1414	826	(161)	—	1012	3348	265	6266	1409
518	162	—	1106	828	(158)	—	1101	3350	69	—	0603
535	(401)	8400	1809	831	(906)	—	2201	3354	(75)	—	0608
563	(204)	—	1207	832	907	—	2202	3364	(843)	6010	1603
564	203	—	1208	833	907	—	2114	3705	(35)	—	0410
598	(928)	—	1111	834	874	—	2204	3731	76	—	—
604	(55)	—	0614	892	28	—	0412	3733	75	—	—
605	(50)	3151	0613	893	27	—	0413	3755	(140)	—	—
611	898	—	2107	899	(27)	3282	0505	3756	158	—	—
612	832	—	2108	904	(258)	6258	1413	3766	167	—	—
644	830	8501	1907	912	209	6225	1212	3768	(922)	—	—
647	(8581)	8900	1813	913	(921)	7051	1711	3772	(379)	—	—
680	901	5374	2210	924	(851)	6008	1706	3779	4146	—	—
702	226	6239	1306	926	(779)	6007	1707				